By the same author

War in Medieval Society (1974)
Borderland (1984)
Lightning Country (1987)
The King of Ashes (1989)
Clay (1989)
The Confirmation (1992)
Y Felan a Finnau (1992)
The City (1993)
Heroes (1996)
No Hiding Place (1996)
Abergavenny (1997)
The Wine Bird (1998)
Ice (2001)
At the Salt Hotel (2003)
Sea Lilies: Selected Poems 1984-2003 (2006)
The Green Buoy (2006)
Trouble in Heaven (2007)
Tales of the Shopocracy (2009)
West Jutland Suite/Vestjysk Suite (2009)
The Forest Under the Sea (2010)
Fire Drill: Notes on the Twenty-First Century (2010)
A Year of Flowers (2011)
The Roaring Boys (2012)
Footfalls in the Silence (2014)
Wind Playing with a Man's Hat (2016)
Departure Lounge (2018)
Sherpas (2018)
Sunglasses (2020)
Afterlives (2021)

A Report to Alpha Centauri

John Barnie

Cinnamon Press
:: small miracles from distinctive voices ::

Published by Cinnamon Press
www.cinnamonpress.com

The right of John Barnie to be identified as author of this work has been asserted by him in accordance with the Copyright, Designs and Patent Act, 1988. © 2021, John Barnie

ISBN 978-1-78864-112-8

British Library Cataloguing in Publication Data. A CIP record for this book can be obtained from the British Library.

All rights reserved. No part of this publication may be reproduced, stored in a retrieval system, or transmitted in any form or by any means, electronic, mechanical, photocopying, recording or otherwise without the prior written permission of the publishers. This book may not be lent, hired out, resold or otherwise disposed of by way of trade in any form of binding or cover other than that in which it is published, without the prior consent of the publishers.

Designed and typeset in Bodoni by Cinnamon Press. Cover design by Adam Craig © Adam Craig from original artwork by Aidan Dullaghan © Aidan Dullaghan..

Cinnamon Press is represented by Inpress

Acknowledgements

'A Report to Alpha Centauri' was commissioned by Sustainable Wales and first appeared on their website. 'The Secret Agent' draws on characters in Conrad's novel.

Note

In 'Near Fforest Coalpit' the word 'idiot' is used advisedly. The poem is based on an incident that occurred in the 1960s, but could have taken place a hundred years earlier.

Contents

To the Reader	13
Lock-step	14
Just Look	15
Old Man Putting Bread Out for the Birds	16
The Circle	17
Sarn y Plas	18
London	19
To the Last Humans	20
At Ease!	21
The Day We Went to Clacton	22
Never Enough	23
Shameful Acts	24
Wish You Were Here	25
Near Fforest Coalpit	26
Consciousness	27
The Secret Agent	28
Witness	34
Ward 4/3	35
Follow the 'Heritage' Sign	38
Washing Day	39
In the Time of Coal	40
Neighbour's Birthday	41
Cracking On	42
To the Directors	43
11.00 Hours	44
Sarn y Plas	45
Future Dreams	46
Nocturne	47
Words	48
Raven-time	49
What Else?	50
The Art of Dining	51
An Optimist to the Birds	52
Getting Through	53
The Green Woodpecker	54
Simple	55
Looking Back Looking Ahead	56

Dogs	57
Part(s) of Nature	58
Listen	59
Ah	60
The Blind Man Speaks	61
What Happened	66
A Report to Alpha Centauri	67

It was one of those dewy, clear, starry nights, oppressing our spirit, crushing our pride, by the brilliant evidence of the awful loneliness, of the hopeless obscure insignificance of our globe lost in the splendid revelation of a glittering, soulless universe.

Joseph Conrad, *Chance*

A Report to Alpha Centauri

To the Reader

These are poems for the times, you don't have to turn them over
they're not George the Third coins with a coppery tarnish
the face bloated, a chaplet of laurel leaves, sagging power of the old days
when lives still threaded the needle's eye of the birth and death

of Jesus Christ; these poems are out there with the chilly wind
and the absence of yellowhammers, with drills and wrecking balls,
you may not want to read them, you may not want to take note,
walking away to the car which you open with an electric key

        saying, not for me.

Lock-step

Adapting to ways of the world
I stay at home as much as I can,
disciples of iPhones digitally dibbing
holding the camera's little eye up
on extendable cranes of hands not
to miss a chance to record a moment
as more moments at a finger-flick
form themselves in excitable pixels
knowing I'm the stranger, the one
walking in the wrong direction
wanting only to see and to touch
not be in touch with half the world
looming selfie faces crowding
to be sure they get in the frame.

Just Look

This robin popping up on top of the hedge
stick legs, heart throbbing, a snatch out of an egg
winter-surviving maybe, if not, one of the shooting stars
that falls to the ground with hardly a sound
the sum of its life no more than an insect's,
no more than ours though we think we're grand
the upright mobile forwardly thinking ape
grabbing a hammer, grabbing a knife,
revving chainsaws in the forest on a frosty morning
rarely thinking there is a universe beyond
eyeless because lifeless, so not seeing itself
as others see us, as we see insects and birds
diminishing around us, ready to throw our hats
on hat-stands, take off our shoes, sit back
in the end-time-easy-recliner, calling it a day.

Old Man Putting Bread Out for the Birds

There's too much trouble in the world;
sorrow's spikes pierce us all; so hobbling out
with bread crumbs on a board to throw

and scatter and bounce in a March wind
is all he can do for now, the birds
distrustful, ready on their feathered quills

to lift back into flight if, after closing the door,
he opens it ajar to watch his uneasy friends
baffled by the barriers evolution placed

between him and them; minutes later the bread
is gone from the lawn's tablecloth when
      he opens the door again.

The Circle

Fingers dovetailed through clumsy gloves
in Upper Pentre Lane in shining frost
she and he two figures of the times below the hills
between hedgerows shepherding their feet, eyes
meeting across billows of breath in the dark;
perhaps there were birds silent and shivering
puffed up with feathers on thin scaly legs
deep in the hedge behind the cast-iron seat
where now they sat in the moon's glare
the town waiting, sure they would come back,
sure they belonged to it, ordinary lovers
wandering to the edge of things, the Rholben
nodding to the Deri, yes, yes, seen before,
walking back along Lower Pentre Lane, circle
complete, town lamps worrying mothers
guiding them home with unnecessary fuss.

Sarn y Plas

Nobody stooping out of the half-stable door
the lean racehorse of a poet has packed up and gone

even if no mathematician he half-knew the score
but wouldn't admit it outside the mind's slate-flagged room

publicly in poems he said Christ was metaphor
many believed him but the best poems are harsh

the waves sweep endlessly in at Porth Neigwl
as he described them breaking on the sand of the shore

far away there are crowds of bobbing faces, restless,
dissatisfied, they jar, demanding always more.

London

Someone must have stirred this termites' nest,
an ape perhaps poking it thoughtfully with a stick,
look at it now, the acidic restlessness, noise,
kinesis made unstoppable by so many humans
metal-shine, angular movement, red amber green

go, parks of shady trees stepped out of
stepped into where there's no fuss but little time
so back onto the streets into the swirl of eyes
arms ears feet pushing the pavements faster;
there is everywhere to get to, nowhere to go.

To the Last Humans

Give your all which is life
accept the waymarkings of a cross
we elaborately built ourselves

hang there pinned by nails
we ourselves hammered in
as our species becomes bones.

At Ease!

Can't remember his name not that it matters
nobody's name is remembered long but he joined the Army
desperate measures from a redbrick council house
came back immaculate to swank about the town
particularly impressive the peaked cap swept low

till it shadowed the face; I'm someone now, watch out
the uniform said, almost pulling me to attention—Sah!
though different on parade no doubt, one more automaton
learning how the be the man, talk about women,
twist bayonets with a lunge to maximise the wound.

The Day We Went to Clacton

I never saw so many English flags
I said to the wife 'it's a foreign country';
the sands were the same, could've been Tenby
gulls diving for burgers
Aber in July

but flags, fluttering everywhere
old Saint George should've been bucked
lager gangs blocked the pavement
'Ingerlund Ingerlund' in your face
Farage's big gob smile
tattoo'd on arms; I said to the wife
'never again';

next year, it's Yr Ysgwrn
to contemplate the Welsh, cheering and dying
for England in her wars.

Never Enough

She was daughter of a bear-keeper
a mediocre one at that
and grew up while the old bear danced
it's a tidy living, you shouldn't complain
the father said
but daughters want to skip and jump, have fine things
want the sun out every day
and that's how it was in the city in the hills
with fir trees and whatnot where I suppose
he captured the bear, a young one
muzzled but old now as I say
when the story begins.

Shameful Acts

If each were a pebble worn smooth by the memory of them
they would pave the shallows of the Usk
by the Castle Meadows or at Llanwenarth
where I could walk across counting with my feet;
it takes a lifetime to cross that simple river

which is not the Mississippi nor the Essequibo
but a country stream, and all the shames
small-town compared to the great shames of the world;
but pebbles are hard and might last a million years
weary lengths of time I do not have.

Wish You Were Here

Let's not be too squeamish about unwritten laws of the universe
or at any rate of Earth
I delight in sunrises, sunsets like anyone else
send picture postcards by the local photographer

'this is where we walked yesterday along stratified cliffs that rose and fell
    in a big dipper
it was the edge of all things
you should have been there

PS tomorrow the Museum to look at carts, billhooks and other discards
though we prefer following the folds and upheavals of the cliffs
the rocks' slow-motion existence
or you might call it concertina, time's squeezebox
playing music we cannot hear'.

Near Fforest Coalpit

I can never forget the idiot nodding to himself
in the little parlour's submarine green
from pot plants I suppose in the tiny window,
rocking as a boulder on a mountain slope
its base cut away by weather but never tumbling
to the valley, descried from far away and told
yes that's the famous rocking stone; I'd
come in looking for the bar, turned left
not right where the old lady with a bearded wart
poured me a splashing pint out of the barrel.

Consciousness

The ragamuffin uninvited
barging past, upsetting tables

the badman looking for alarm
in other creatures' eyes.

The Secret Agent

*She felt profoundly that things
do not stand much looking into.*

Stott-Wartenheim

Baron Stott-Wartenheim, how do you do?
we've never met
I know you by reputation from a novel I've read
several times you crop up as somebody past it
too Old School for the business of the day
I imagine this is so
rummaging in dirty stuff of explosions, agents provocateurs
doesn't fit with a rose garden, unmarried daughters
who I made up
but they seem appropriate
what do you think, did you have some
plump around the middle
and on a shelf so ample they still half-hope
ready to cwtsh if the right man comes along
or any man at all.

Chief Inspector Heat

Braces off
smoked haddock for tea
fish smell lingering through the room
what's for pudding
roly poly of course
the wife certainly knows how to treat a man well
plate pushed back
for tobacco and pipe
nothing to compare with domestic retreat
the night's soft pillow
the wife a looming but not annoying presence
sleep dreamless as death
that's what a man wants
to make existence complete
wouldn't you say, Heat?

Cabman

Here comes the cabman
don't know his name, let's call him Joe
if there was a gauge for life
it would hover on 'Empty'
he tried to explain to that half-witted kid
the horse heading for the knackers
but no, got off at the alms houses
and Joe came here to suck up a pint;
another day almost gone, Joe,
aye-aye he says to himself
while life passes by on the street
a blaze of canaries.

The Great Personage

If it's important to be important
this man knows it best
I never met him of course
circles within circles within circles
the very thought of shaking his hand
makes me dizzy
I can't believe he goes to the toilet
getting up from the 'vitreous washdown'
drying his hands

big stars are forming
the House will sit all night.

Karl Yundt

Old Karl Yundt
if he found a thre'penny bit
would dance on his sticks
that's what a revolutionary's lean years
bring a man to
help him out of the shop
where porno sales
are slow tonight.

Brett Street

Do you know
you'll never believe it
but I've lived in streets like this
brick walls
windows where the frames are rotten
landlady
in a ground-floor room
coming out to take the rent on Friday
a glimpse of the stuffed and cluttered life
she'll leave one day
like we all do
in an undertaker's box.

Lady-Wife

The Assistant Commissioner's lady-wife
doesn't fool me one bit
those rouged lips, flushed cheeks
varnished nails, lahdidah
ew reahlly!
talk of the Salong
where she meets fraightfully
interesting people
how he puts up with it
we'll never know

a quiet ex-colonial man
much too good for her
shot a man-eater in Burma
or Bengal
some say why not shoot her
but I never like that kind of talk.

Lodgers

A cardboard suitcase
is a statement of failure
not for carrying bare necessities
but a life folded up,
it doesn't matter how many times
you lay it out on a cold-sprung bed
grinning in the mirror
at a good set of teeth, be reasonable,
anyone could end like this.

The Professor

What a head
it should be in a collection
padlocked like his cupboard
at night he dreamed of a tower of skulls
reaching to the clouds
move over Professor
or is there room for only one
on the narrow plank of your bed.

Night Patrol

PCs come and go
but look the same
walking down Brett Street

trying doors
noticing the shop's
shut early, lights
at the back
rattling the lock
longing to say you're nicked my son
though no one was arrested
for the Brett Street affair.

Mrs Neale

Mrs Neale the skivvy
what would she make of the upturned hat
life's begging bowl where nobody
casts a penny in
surrounded by blood
on the lino
useless to ask, just another task
after police had taken the body away
swab swab swab, water
turning pink in the pail
so, Mrs Neale, how was your day?

Extra! Extra!

Except it wasn't,
just a column Ossipon
lighted upon, a lonely woman's
casting herself in the sea
a mystery;
watch that double-page spread's
undulating skate wings
in a scuff of wind
don't trap it with a foot
the past can burn.

Bit Parts

The tick tick tick tick of blood
dripping out isn't a clock
but a flood on the ebb
never to return,
just like the knife
used to stab two
hearts as it turned out
one drowning in cold waves
as the ferry's Wurlitzer
steamed on

bit parts
we're all bit parts
one way or another.

Witness

I couldn't believe it, 'kick his head in'
the woman in heels screamed, bending
as the skirt slid up her thighs, and he did,

the fallen man a rolling dog in Pompeii
covered by burning ash, 'kick him',
the misery of a downtown street at night.

Ward 4/3

Last Chance

The automatic voice sounds tired
doors, opening ... doors, closing
day after day, night after night
amidst the rubble of humanity

brought here to see what doctors
can do in a confidence of white coats
even when they shake their heads
doors, opening ... doors, closing.

Visiting Hours

Time has been trapped under a bell jar, ticking furiously
            that terrible insect,
                        the inmates, like yesterday's sandwiches
nobody wants to buy, propped or lying prone
            in washed-out rags of skin left to air
                        on clothes-horses of bone,
telephones keep ringing
            there must be some urgency
                        but everything is calm,
life dwindled to a fly
            alighting on a table where a spilled drink's lake
                        reflects the ceiling.

Nappies

'Why don't these people learn how to cook?'
it's the old man in the next bed, he doesn't like the food,
doesn't like nappies either, but there it is,

they've all got one, the grizzled babies who, as Tom said,
ought to be explorers but are not, not now, not on
the bleak side of this moon where Zimmer frames

are the moonmobiles they use to inch toward the toilets,
gravity being heavy here; don't think all moons
are a hop-skip-and-a-jump like the one in the sky.

An Unusual Species

Dried up and disappointed like a river bed,
though fish eggs may blow about in dust
in caked-up mud to spring fully-fashioned into life
at the least of the rains because time and death
have stopwatches and in this insignificant pool

there is a chance to quiver and breed, laying eggs
to wait in the between-times of drought
for clouds and the chance to start again, but
not here on Ward 4/3, old men laid in rows
on banks of white beds where rain never comes.

Break-Out

ESCAPE OF THE GERIATRICS—headline news
there they go, white chickens in hospital clothes
under the wire, fanning out across muddy fields
staggering confused, straggling in ones and threes
safari-park bewildebeests at the edge of town

how it ended, don't worry, nurses rounded them up
'come along now'—not too severe because of the law
seen from a drone it could have been prophets
assembled for enlightenment, a gathering of druids
'oes heddwch?' 'nac oes' this side of the graves.

Coming Away from the Hospital

Why did they give me his teeth?
did he slip them in because he had last advice?

gums pink as a little girl's party dress
with a saliva gleam

divorced from the mouth's clapper-claw
what use? they wouldn't frighten mice

couldn't tell the crows a joke
wrapped in a dressing gown, the conjuror's

world-famous last-minute trick;
why did they give me his teeth?

Follow the 'Heritage' Sign

Have you been to the refrigerator dump
it's well worth it, piled drunkenly high
some doors shut some swung open
always a swirl of gulls as if refrigerated

and just released to wheel and jabber;
it reminds me of Easter Island, great projects
abandoned, and who the people were
pulling on the rubber seal for morning milk

shutting it with a quiet slap no one
now can say; the dump is best seen in sun
a bright white jumbled pyramid erected
as a victory mark or memorial of defeat.

Washing Day

What was it about Mondays
dirty clothes bundled downstairs
dumped with contempt for a prisoner's cast-offs
in corrugated tubs, drowned with dollies
twirled in ballroom-dancing classes
dollies' prongs poking and jeering
as the clothes swam up

the mangle's indifference
sheets flattened in creases
led by hand to a basket below
pegs old as nursery rhymes
raised in hallelujahs to a drying wind
clamping clothes to the line
the grand hoisting of props.

In the Time of Coal

It came from over the mountain but we didn't go there
to the row-house streets that had no cars
and lean men with a hostile look,
hands-in-pockets-country during a strike
or pickets-of-anger seen on the News;

and Nye Bevan in the Market Hall the prophet
come among us with thunderous words
to blow the bourgeois shopkeepers away
pillaging the rich in Avenue Road, sweeping
their lives' detritus down the Usk through
the jeers of Newport to the sea.

Neighbour's Birthday

You stand in the shadow cast by time
steadily approaching across the lawn
the guest you forgot about
holding the string of a yellow balloon
waiting outside the cellophane blackness of the windows
watching us there with plates and glasses
listening to the scrabble of our chatter.

Cracking On

Already practising to be an old man? that's unacceptable
whip yourself like the wind does the trees

it doesn't matter to them that twigs and leaves are torn away
strewn in the path in the deep lane

give yourself a good talking to; why
I've seen an old larch on Skirrid Fach torn up with vertical roots

cluttered with stones and earth, and dead you'd think
but among the smashed branches fresh shoots of green

a struggling up and struggling on;
Death had to take a break, this tree was too great for him.

To the Directors

Gentlemen, the pole dancers have retired for the night
the electronic banks hum and glow

think of the stars, the waste of energy
harness that, become the immortals

think of the moon, consolidated mines
the uplands of Mars

here on Earth the deserts have never recovered
the universe is a cloth of gold.

11.00 Hours

There's a time to bomb and a time to pray
    bombing is preying
        but note the change of vowel

how can we camouflage our disguises
    coming out of church
        thanking the vicar

poppies make bright winter wreaths
    and wreath is close to wraith,
        but no wraiths here

just the statue of a soldier
    rifle butt to the ground
        looking wearily at the town.

Sarn y Plas

Peered in windows at emptiness
where mice used to watch and listen

to fingers raised above typewriter keys
conducting a poem into the world

to be a conductor of many little things
to be a builder who brick by brick

raised a building of poems then left
shutting the door without looking back.

Future Dreams

Let's say we did terraform Mars
    what then?
        I can see shores of the Great Sea

hear children's squeals in the sky
    gulls' shadows sweeping over sand,
        'this is the life',

'don't you think there's always a worm in the apple?
    don't you think it would follow us here?'
        'pesimista' they'd say in the lingua franca

settling in deck chairs,
    spotting Earth after the sun hid its blinkless eye
        under the horizon.

Nocturne

Looking at a satellite photograph of Earth at night
we've turned it, I see, into a map of lights
except Africa, Himalaya, one or two places more
that haven't got there yet; a xylophone of the bizarre

you want to reach out for your hammers and play
silvery music sparkling gaiety, its twinkling
absorbed with a rush by deep space where
there's no music and stars illuminate nothing.

Words

You have to give praise to words
how you can throw up their little mice bones
to fill a whole sky
to watch the patter of their fall
poets and novelists try to capture them alive
rarely winning because words can play dead
page after page, you'll find them in every second hand bookshop

poor words, you say, they could be so *vivant*
but have no shine; words unlike writers
have second lives, even thirds or fourths,
a dictionary is a bulging mouth crammed with words
a cobbler with nails sprouting between lips
taken out patiently
to hammer in a perfect heel.

Raven-time

Frost, snow and a hard winter
hills of the Black Mountains white mainsails
in a white sea, the great ship
heaving over the town, a humanity-huddle
banking up fires, leaving cars to run
with pale smoking twirls of exhaust
snow crisp as ice under wellington'd feet
breath-clouds, and if you climbed the Deri
on and on among waves of white, a raven for company
though how it survives nobody knows.

What Else?

Foxes dancing on the street in Mumbles
I wouldn't have believed it in grey urban dawn
the prancing delight of the wild withheld
from our civilised eyes and desperate too
with lean hunger tipping out dustbins

foxes like to play, scamper in the world
just like us when we forget how lonely
a universe of galaxies can be, finger pressed
to the pulse of the flow of life, feeling its beat
whispered advice to be glad in ourselves.

The Art of Dining

Well here's a Neanderthal Mousterian knife
but where's the fork? only joking; King Richard the Second
was the first, wasn't he, to deploy such measures

at grand feasts in the royal hall, flourishing one
while the dinner guests stared, wondering what it was;
Neanderthals, of course, were unknown then;

what would courtiers have made of a prognathous jaw;
it's Cain, naturally, the first killer who prowled Earth
taking the rap, unwilling to leave life's savagery to God.

An Optimist to the Birds

You have no idea of the extent of human desire,
it reaches beyond the mouths of babies and the coffin's bevelled edges
to that tiny pinprick or flash or whatever it was
that began it all and into the core of the sun and the deserts of Mars,

into the wastes of Io; beyond and beyond the mind spans
and if we ever have to cry 'is there nothing left to know'
it will be the end, the pneumatic drills will fall silent
chainsaws left propped against the boles of giant trees;

I can't believe it will happen, human means travelling on,
there can never be a terminus of concrete walls,
the bruised hand at the table lifting the cup, the mouth drinking,
the sun climbing triumphantly to overlook us in the sky.

Getting Through

Each autumn a descent to a cellar dank with apples
pleasing, that end-of-year smell of waxy fruit
but not what follows, winter being a harsh misfortune,

the house a submarine running silent, television
our periscope onto the world as we flick to the news, more
wildfires in California, I see, a town called Ashland

filled with smoke, war in Sudan, starvation in Yemen, *down
periscope* the order is given, we've seen enough, climbing stairs
to rest for a while on the seabed of another night.

The Green Woodpecker

To this undulating wonder—flying
from Rholben's bright oak wood
to Deri's oak-sprawled slopes
across the sunlit space of the Vale
green the trees, green the grass
green the bracken but greenest
by my reckoning this woodpecker
glimpsed as a flash of hummingbird
in a Guyanese garden on the edge
of dark forests, green lit by the sun
celebrated, a fistful of joy flung
from wood to wood and nothing
now left, neither feather nor bone
except in this memory—praise.

Simple

There's no beginning or end to this
but I must tell you about the bar-tailed godwits
who when they turned in flight
showed autumn in rufous feathers
yet were so alive in transit along the sands
and then on, on beyond the terrestrial
nature of our lives and the dog
that barked and chased and barked
happy with the expression of its being.

Looking Back Looking Ahead

You can't get sparks out of a dead fire
that's it, it's gone
with the rest of a day to get through
night when owls are Easter Islands
because we've done for them
'excuse me' you'll say 'haven't we the right to exist'
of course, yes, and of course, no,
nothing has rights that I've heard of

it's too far-fetched; three-point-eight-billion years ago
the map was sketched, the as-it-is plan
for what came after;
and it will go on like this;
once the cleaver is out of the drawer
it's chop-chop-chop to the end of the story.

Dogs

The Earth is going to the dogs but the dogs don't care,
they'd rather have a walk on an extendable lead
with all the excitable smells pulling them on, or a tickle behind the ear,
or a dish of mashed-up slobbery guff to bury their nose in,
everything is life to them until Oblivion drops a stone on their head,

this comes as a surprise of course, dogs never having worked it out,
running with a ball to drop at your feet passing as foresight,
lapping a bowl of water, chasing gulls on the beach at Ynys-las,
that scampering bound of floppy ears, paws plashing in wet sand,
until whistled back, they fling themselves into the four-by-four.

Part(s) of Nature

You say humanity, I say barbarity,
where does the Blind Judge sit in this

no good asking on a January morning
as the boldest blackbird hop-skips away
but doesn't fly before the man who brings gifts
of fuel for its jumpiest life so it may
bull-charge other blackbirds for the best mate
and be triumphant in Spring; at breakfast

the man reads the news; breakdown of talks
another massacre, foreign exchange rate
up or down depending; other birds appear,

dislodge the blackbird, bigger, bolder
rooks and crows reaching for the crown.

Listen

Why not give it back to the animals and birds
I've seen the sign NOT WANTED HERE
written in poisoned waters of the old canal
carved on pavements, sprayed on city walls

there are middens wherever we have been
showing the cheapness of it all because
moving on is part of what we are; *mistake!*
it rings through the air a great bell tolling.

Ah

I walked in winter along forest trails
fir trees dripping condensation
spring-heeled on layers of needles
and deep within the dark impenetrable
roe deer eyes, grace watching clumsy;
look I have no gun, but who knows,
gloved hands may hide intent the deer
cannot see, so crash off deeper
or dissolve, eyes disappearing pools
in forest gloom; great grey shrikes
spike helpless food on thorns; a black
woodpecker with a red crown
flings itself reckless between trees;
never so alive, each puff of breath
expelled from pistons of the flesh.

The Blind Man Speaks

In a dark time, the eye begins to see.
                    Theodore Roethke

We Should Talk About It

The last helicopter, though we didn't know it at the time,
took off with a wave and a smile from the pilot's dental-flossed teeth
have-a-good-day-have-a-good-day the blades seemed to say
as they *putter-putter-puttered* into thinning distance like an artist
who began by drawing a solid straight line then lost interest

letting his hand carry on as he looked away; have a good day
while the blue sky was empty, no transatlantic business flights
or rock-bottom holiday crowds singing *here-we-go*; look
instead at a fox jumping up, Lazarus-alive among the sere
coarse winter grass where it had been sunning itself,

a heart-thumping flash into brush to avoid what might be
this destroying intruder; animals have no Saviour and never had,
no Eden for them to be thrown out of, only for humans
who afterwards discovered there was nowhere to go, asking too late
who fixed the arrowhead onto the shaft, with resin and twine,

            who strung the bow.

Restricted Areas

Grass can still be grown in restricted areas
where each Spring a few tatterdemalion sheep
bring forth lambs which is good, which is pleasing
because innocence has become a synonym with us
for Fool's Gold to be trampled in the megacities

where crowds press and hurry in the streets,
where fighter planes have the grace of antique birds
spindly-legged with minute brains allowing them to do
the one thing, though for now at rest at the edge
of shimmering runways, and pilots laughing and yawning

wondering when it will all begin so they can trash
the air's silk; as I say, grass in sheltered well-watered places
can still be grown and schools take children there
to pet the lambs and run and chase like lambs themselves
our new-borns soon to grow up and look about a world

> where lambs lie without tongues or eyes
> because we have made it so.

Tar

I must say presidents and others give a good show,
the ones we say we invented and put in power
through magical voting after forcing them to reveal
how sincere they are—and they are—sincere as banks
their pantries where they stack conserves for tomorrow

not worrying about the odd five pence that rolls
out of the door onto the street; born to command or not
they flank themselves with carefully folded flags
'you and I together are the nation', though half the nation
hates them and the other half hates that half in turn

elections being a bubbling tarry lake which anyone
who seeks to bathe in becomes a tarry tale themselves
easily feathered by the Press and run out of the People's Town
onto a jet which takes them to a rich man's hideaway;
what will take tar off, what will make it unstick from a name

> that once shone in a mother's eye
> like a five-pence piece.

The Floating City

'And tears started from his pillow in the sky'
the end of a story my mother told me I remember now
in the fourth year of drought; but I am deflected
from what I had to say about the floating city built
on rubbish in a broad lagoon; what to do with rubbish

it has to go somewhere, the city authorities deciding
this was the spot, rubbish bulldozed into soggy water
smothering white sand, cascading through sunlight
farther out and deeper down; rats saw their chance
the first day, and humans followed because the poor

live where they have to and where they can, shanties
almost rubbish themselves built on narrow winding lanes
children in rags with wideawake stares of the hungry
and sometimes a gentle undulation as if the shanty put to sea
so quietly you hardly noticed, if you lived there, or cared

      what voyage you were on.

Famished

Then there was the mother gorilla and beside her
her little child, the mother standing up to stare
at humans staring back as if neither knew what to do
or how to introduce themselves, conversationally awkward
with no mutual gambits they could try, except

the mother had something in her hand folded softly
until she opened it on a bolus of dark green ordure
she had carefully warmed and preserved to show
to anyone curious enough to stop before the glass;
'life is like this in a concrete cage with a wall of glass',

the message was clear if wordless, words getting in the way
of the profoundest truths; that was before raids on the zoo
led to bushmeat riots—I remember them well, as do you—
skin-deep our respect as animals were dragged screaming
into the slaughterhouse of real life, cars speeding away

    with glistening parcels of flesh.

The Song

The song is quiet, it harms no one, on a day like this
when lilacs are displaying their rich pink flowers smothering
the senses with the colour of scent and two butterflies
speckled woods I believe, tangle and untangle with each other
in a dizzy light exuberance then disappear to take their wrangle

to another garden, even the sky is an outpouring of blue
and the sun acts as if there is only kindness anywhere in the universe
and although it isn't true we choose to believe it because today
we push back our clouds to the horizon wanting for once a new life
the chance of happiness, not wanting the vortex tumbling us round

faster and faster than the Wall of Death at a small town funfair
not wanting to know that things will not end well for us or for babies
in hospital rows with milky vague eyes and rose-tip buds for fingers
an all-feeling, all-helpless event in our lives we cannot remember
for ourselves and cannot help in others who have to be born

    because the life-flush is strong.

The Wound

Have you been to the city sinking through caverns
of the dried-out aquifer, the streets making cruel
approximations to waves and the cathedral where the Crown
looks wobbly but not the Thorns and cars meander in S's
around sinkholes where we can see the past is deep

though not the future which is a concrete wall economists
say just isn't there; how long can we continue with the Sin
of being Ourselves; I too have seen the old man
tottering with a stick, crying 'Mother Earth, let me in';
how long has he been doing the rounds; Chaucer

saw him, I believe, as he wandered in the fields in Spring
after the latest battle where eagles and ravens straddled the slain;
that is the cry now, turning from Christ's sorrowful face
and Mary weeping, who were only pinpricks in the fabric of time
that unwound like a prisoner's bandage from the wound

       we inflicted on ourselves.

What Happened

This is no time for rhyme so poets stopped scribbling
looked in mirrors at change in themselves
faced the unfaceable—words hanging shrivelled on the vines.

A Report to Alpha Centauri

INITIALLY I was reluctant to enter solar system S-23-44. Long-range scans indicated gas giants and rocky planets with either no atmosphere or a poisonous one. There was one exception, however, S-23-44-3, which our bio-scientists thought worth investigation.

This planet, third from the star, has a breathable atmosphere. Broadly speaking, there are three zones, the poles, a northern and a southern temperate zone, and an equatorial zone. At the north pole there is an extensive ocean; at the south a barren rocky landmass. The temperate zone is arid, vegetation being limited to grass and low scrub. The equatorial zone, however, is covered with dense tropical forests containing abundant fauna. This luxuriance is due to the high level of carbon sequestration by the forests and the resultant release of large volumes of oxygen into the atmosphere.

Interestingly, the body plans of the fauna are familiar to us from Alpha Centauri 3. This has led our bio-scientists to hypothesise that the 'design space' available to carbon-based life may be limited, resulting in evolutionary 'convergence' on planets thousands of light years apart. If true, this would have profound scientific, not to say philosophical, implications.

What can be said with a high degree of certainty is that there is no intelligent life on S-23-44-3. Given the profusion of species in the equatorial zone which must have taken millions of years to evolve, this prompts a further speculation, that intelligence is a rare commodity in our galaxy, far rarer than the optimists would have us believe.

There are, however, two anomalies which puzzle me. One is an elusive forest creature, a specimen of which we captured. It is of medium height and covered in sparse, coarse, dark hair. I cannot say it walks, but it travels along the ground propelling itself with its hind legs while supporting its weight on the knuckles of its hands. The hands have opposable thumbs. For some of the time it lives in the forest canopy where it appears to be equally at home.

The specimen we captured is a young male. When I look into its brown eyes I seem to see a glimmer of intelligence, as if it is considering me. It does not have the faculty of speech, however, and we are unable to communicate with it. Opposable thumbs mean it can grasp objects easily and in theory ought to be able to use tools. This has not yet been observed in the wild or in captivity, but I would not rule it out.

Could this be the dawn of intelligent life on S-23-44-3? If so, what might we find if we returned in 5 million years? It is an intriguing question. On leaving we will kill it and preserve the cadaver for further analysis.

I mentioned two anomalies. The second is in many ways the more interesting but also the more resistant to interpretation.

In the northern temperate zone our geo-scientists examined a sea cliff 120m high, composed of red sandstone overlain with 30m of mudstone. Nothing unusual in this, of course. The sandstone is estimated to be 130 million years old plus or minus, while the overlying mudstone accumulated between 10 and 5 million years ago. What attracted the geo-scientists' attention was a narrow band 2m thick and 50m wide at the intersection of the formations. Analysis revealed that it is composed of a coarse granite gravel mixed with sand, calcium silicates, and traces of aluminium and iron. It was light grey in colour and stood out clearly against the reds and browns of the surrounding strata.

The geo-scientists assure me that this combination of rocks, minerals and metals is unique in their experience, so much so that they are convinced it is not a natural formation. What then is it? How far does it extend inland beneath the mudstone? And the biggest question of all: if it is not natural then it must be artificial, which implies a maker of considerable intelligence. Yet we have found no other evidence to suggest there has ever been intelligent life on the planet. Granted that this structure (if that is what it is) is circa 10 million years old, and granted that most traces of a civilisation, even an advanced one, would have disappeared between then and now, surely some clues would remain as to who had built it and why?

I look into the eyes of the forest creature in his cage, and he looks into mine. Almost, I feel, he is telling me something, then he turns away. Large butterflies glide through the clearing we have made in the forest, invisible animals and birds scream and call from the canopy. I have decided not to kill the creature. When we depart tomorrow I shall let it go, shambling off on its knuckles like some half-completed being.

The creature turns from the fruit it has been eating, its hands grasping the bars. We gaze into each other's eyes, and for a moment I see... but I cannot say... like the creature, it seems, I suddenly have no words. I put out a hand and gently touch one of his. Then the moment is gone. Once again there is only the silence between us.

I will be glad to leave this planet. It is a world of shadows, a world—though I know this sounds strange, even as I write it down—of ghosts. Something happened here a long time ago, I am certain; something glorious, and something terrible. I can feel it; I can see it in the forest creature's eyes. Yes, I will be glad to be leaving. This planet disturbs me with its silences. It is not recommended for colonisation. We will not be coming back.